LEARN ABOUT PAGANISM

Yule

WITH
Grani Hulda

Pagan Books for Pagan Kids

Grani Hulda

This book
belongs to:

_____

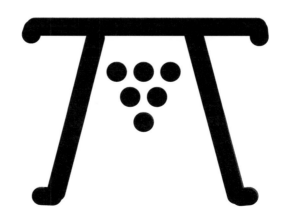

What is Yule?

Yule is the Winter Solstice, which is when Winter officially begins.

It is the shortest day of the year. At Yule, pagans celebrate the return of the light.

It is the longest night of the year. After Yule, the light increases and the days start getting longer.

The Holly King surrenders to the Oak King at Yule.

The Oak King will soon return to power.

For now, it is cold and the nights are long and dark.

The Return of the Light

At Yule, the Sun is getting more powerful.
The Sun promises that it will be warm again

To honor the promise of the Sun, Grani Hulda lights candles at Yule. Only adults should light candles, and they must be very careful with them.

Yule season is a time to be with family.

Grani Hulda decorates with evergreen tree branches and pinecones, which are symbols of everlasting life.

Evergreen wreaths are an ancient symbol of eternal life. Circles and wheels show how everything keeps going, forever and ever.

The Yule Log is burning every night for 12 nights at Yule.

Yule is Grani Hulda's favorite time to read.

Yule is also a good time for pagans to cast runes and read tarot cards.

Celebrate Yule

There are many ways to celebrate Yule.

Grani Hulda is busy cooking, baking and decorating her home for the Yule Feast.

Yule is a time to do nice things for others. At Yule, Grani Hulda makes toys for children.

Grani Hulda gives presents to her animal friends at Yule.

Grani Hulda celebrates Yule by decorating an altar.

A Yule altar is a good way to honor the Gods and Goddesses and show our gratitude for the abundance in our lives.

Evergreen trees remind us that our spirits are everlasting.

Merry Yule!

Made in United States
Troutdale, OR
11/11/2024